1000

JOURNAL PROMPTS THAT WILL TRANSFORM

YOUR HEALTH

Sophia Ley

Copyright © 2019 by Sophia Ley

www.elevateyourdiet.com

CONTENTS

Introduction..7

Benefits of Journaling 9

How To Use These Journal Prompts 11

Eye Opening Prompts To Improve Your

Relationship With Food 13

Observant Prompts That Lead To Deeper Self

Awareness 19

Life Changing Prompts To Inspire A Healthier

Lifestyle...27

Insightful Prompts To Level Up Your Nutrition

Knowledge...37

Moving Prompts That Activate Energy And

Activity..49

Powerful Prompts That Spark Self Care 59

Effective Prompts For Clarity in Overcoming

Setbacks..67

Uplifting Prompts That Increase Happiness

Through Gratitude..73

Thoughtful Prompts For Culture And Weight

Bias 81

Conclusion...87

INTRODUCTION

"A personal journal is an ideal environment in which to "become". It is a perfect place for you to think, feel, discover, expand, remember and dream." —Brad Wilcox

Hello and welcome to 1000 Journal Prompts That Will Transform Your Health. I'm Sophia and it's wonderful to meet you!

As a nutritionist practicing in the field of nutritional psychology, I am obsessed with the mind body connection.

Did you know that when it comes to your health, diet and exercise is not the end all and be all?

Your mind plays a monumental role in getting diet and exercise to fall into place, yet your mind is the most neglected part of the picture when it comes to health and weight loss.

In over 10 years of practice, I've helped hundreds of women achieve their health goals by incorporating the power of the mind into their weight loss plans.

This is a collection of the thought provoking questions prompts and nudges I've professionally used to help women overcome the main stumbling blocks that are keeping them from achieving their goals.

Your mind is the missing link to the solutions you've been looking for. Keep your mind healthy and you hold the key to long term weight loss without sacrificing an ideal lifestyle.

BENEFITS OF JOURNALING

Several scientific studies have shown that keeping a journal is a useful tool for aiding weight loss. It's effective for understanding your behaviors and powerful for encouraging change. It brings you closer to the root of the challenges you're facing, often in great detail.

Journaling provides insights to solutions you may never have considered, or understood previously. The act of journaling also helps you get inner-critic talk out of your head and onto paper so it can be handled more productively.

You'll see with reflection, what your patterns are and how you can make change for good. You can visualize and look back on the things you wouldn't have seen, unless you look at it over a period of time.

Through journaling, you really get a chance to reflect on what worked, what didn't and why. There are so many other benefits of journaling, only some of which are listed below.

Remove Judgement. Journaling provides a way to address all of your feelings without having to censor your thoughts. It's a helpful way to get everything off your chest without judgement.

Inner Peace. The act of writing lets you take the time necessary to calm your feelings and think twice about acting irrationality. Letting the paper absorb your words is a therapeutical way to stay calm and connected to your higher being.

Solutions. These prompts are designed to get you to think outside your comfort zone. As you write, you'll inevitably start to come up with solutions to some of the roadblocks keeping you from your ideal health.

Perspective. Journaling offers a deeper glimpse into your mind. It helps you understand why you react to things the way you do. The more honest you are in your writing, the more perspective you gain.

Accountability. When you're working towards health and happiness, journaling has the added benefit of keeping you accountable. Tracking your habits, working through the obstacles you encounter, and formulating plans to reach your goals will have a positive impact on your success.

Patterns. Keeping a written log of your health patterns can help you identify certain trends over time. You may notice triggers that unveil patterns of overeating, or stressors that cause mindless munching. The trick is to write it all down and reflect back on your journal entries periodically to see what insights you can gain.

HOW TO USE THESE JOURNAL PROMPTS

The more detail you are able to to put into your journaling entries, the better.

These prompts are meant to get your mind to open to new possibilities and really challenge some of the beliefs you have about yourself and your health. They're meant to bring forth the hidden challenges that are holding you back, so you can overcome them.

Use your private journal as a time to be completely honest with yourself. This is the only way you can get rid of your limiting beliefs and let your ideal self shine through.

Prompts usually start with a simple and minimal statements or question. As they are just prompts, used to gain insight and delve deeper, be sure to open the gates of possibility by asking WHY for each prompt you choose and elaborate as much as you can.

Many of the prompts will nudge you in the direction of doing more research, or obtaining information that's vital to your well being.

Some of the questions might seem repetitive or redundant, that's because different people respond to different prompts. Use the one that most speaks to you and gets you thinking and excited about what's to come.

Since awareness and reflection are the most important part of your health journal, be sure to look back and review what you wrote.

The goal is to bring forth vibrance and abundance to help you live your healthiest, most fulfilling life. Let's ignite love, joy, gratitude and vitality by making the mind body connections necessary to create harmony between health and your chosen lifestyle.

EYE OPENING PROMPTS TO IMPROVE YOUR RELATIONSHIP WITH FOOD

"The bond between food and me is like other relationships in my life: complicated, evolving, demanding, and in need of constant work. But together we've come so far, moving from childhood obligation to clean my plate, to a mindless need to fill up, to a truly nourishing and pleasurable exchange. That's the real reward." —Ashley Graham

1. What do I want food to do for me — deeply at the core?

2. Are my choices leading to my wholeheartedness, or do they leave me feeling empty and searching?

3. Am I making my food choices out of love or something else?

4. If I was acting out of self love, instead of fear of change, how would my actions be different?

5. What is my inner critic telling me specifically before, during, and after eating?

6. Is there a certain time of day or physical location where I binge or feel intense cravings?

7. Is my current pattern of eating bringing me closer-to or farther- from my goals?

8. When I was 12, my relationship with food could be described as...

9. What am I craving in life that I'm using food to fulfill?

10. What are the thoughts going through my head when I eat "junk food"?

11. What are the thoughts that are going through my head after I've eaten something I'm "not supposed" to eat?

12. How do I feel after I binge?

13. Sometimes, I justify stuffing my face by telling myself the following...

14. If I eat when I'm not physically hungry it's because...

15. I haven't reached out for support due to my emotional eating because...

16. I feel most connected when ...

17. What is the biggest stressor in my life that may contribute to using food as a coping mechanism?

18. When I look in the mirror, what do I see?

19. What parts of my life will be different if I lose weight?

20. Weight matters to me because...

21. If I eat to cope, where does the stress go?

22. When I was a child, my parents or caregivers, when talking about my body, used to say...

23. When I was a child, my parents or caregivers, when talking about my eating habits used to say...

24. What did I learn about my body from my mother?

25. If I could snap my fingers and make it happen, my relationship with food would look like...

26. The times where able to choose healthy, nourishing food could be described as...

27. What are all the good things that I know about food?

28. What are all the bad things I know about food?

29. In what way is food good?

30. Is food bad? Why?

31. What are my food triggers?

32. How/why are my cravings triggered?

33. What usually happens when I'm trying to lose weight but I get a craving?

34. What should I do when I get a craving?

35. Are you a stress eater?

36. What constitutes stress eating?

37. How do you deal with stress in a non food way?

38. How can I manage my emotions so they don't get out of hand?

39. What makes me feel in control of my health?

40. What makes me feel out of control when it comes to my health?

41. What was I eating the last time I overate?

42. Why did I overeat?

43. How did I feel the last time I overate?

44. How do I wish I felt about food?

45. List all the foods that make you feel bad.

46. Why do I eat?

47. What 3 words describe my relationship with food right now?

48. What 3 words do I wish describe my relationship with food?

49. If my emotional eating has a message, what is it trying to tell me?

50. What are my biggest daily challenges with my body?

51. What do I feel stressed about? What do I do with these feelings?

52. What do I feel guilty about? What do I do with these feelings?

53. What do I feel angry about? What do I do with these feelings?

54. What do I feel joyous about? How can replicate these feelings?

55. What do I feel abundant about? How can replicate these feelings?

56. I feel most at peace and connected when I... because...

57. What advice would I give to younger me about food?

58. What advice would I give to older me about food?

59. What would it mean if I were "good enough?"

60. When I think of my body, the first thought that pops into my head is...because...

61. Am I obsessed with food?

62. What would my life be like without my obsession with food?

63. What would my life be like without my obsession about my body?

64. If fat could talk it would say...

65. If my body could talk, it would tell me...

66. How does sadness feel in my body?

67. What does happiness feel like in my body?

68. Is my body happy? What are people's first impressions of me?

69. What do I want my first impression to be?

70. What are some regrets I have?

71. What are some past events I just can't get past?

72. How would it feel to let go of bad experiences?

73. What is my biggest worry at the moment?

74. Can I control the things I worry about?

75. What are 3 small actions I can take to help me get less stressed?

76. What are all the things I should not be worrying about?

77. What are all the things that don't matter in life?

78. If I died today, would I be happy with my life and the type of person am I?

79. What is the most dominant emotion in my life right now?

80. Am I happy with my current health habits?

81. Are my choices comforting and nourishing my spirit, or are they temporary reprieves from vulnerability and difficult emotions ultimately diminishing my spirit?

82. What is something positive that's come out of a negative experience?

83. Write a letter to someone you have a grudge against and end it with "I forgive you".

84. What patterns or understandings can I see about my relationship with emotional eating?

OBSERVANT PROMPTS THAT LEAD TO DEEPER SELF AWARENESS

"By becoming self aware, you gain ownership of reality; in becoming real, you become the master of both inner and outer life." —Deepack Chopra

85.   10 reasons why I want to lose weight.

86.   What is my most compelling reason for losing weight?

87.   10 things I really love about my body

88.   Name at least 10 good things about your personality.

89.   What is your inner beauty?

90.   How many sizes of clothes do you have in your closet?

91.   How do your "skinny" clothes make you feel?

92.   Why do you keep your "fat" clothes?

93.   What would happen if I gave away every piece of clothing that didn't fit me?

94.   Describe the experience you had the last time you went shopping for clothes.

95.   Describe the last shopping trip you had that was a positive experience.

96.   Describe the last shopping trip you had that was a bad experience.

97. Describe in detail the thoughts and feelings you had as you purchased the last time you were "skinny"

98. When I look in the mirror I see...

99. When I look in the mirror I feel...

100. List all the positive things that people around you have said to you.

101. List all the things people around you have said to you that you were sensitive to.

102. Do you think you have poor body image? Why?

103. Do you think you have depression due to your weight? What are you doing about it?

104. Do you think you have low self esteem due to your weight? What can you do about it?

105. List ways you can heal your body image issues.

106. List things you're doing to maintain a positive attitude about your body and appearance.

107. What does body positivity mean to you?

108. Have you ever experienced discrimination for being the size you are? Describe what happened.

109. What role did your mother have in your feelings about yourself and your shape?

110. What role did the other women in your family have in feelings about yourself and your shape?

111. What older women are role models for you now?

112. What comments have you gotten from romantic partner/spouses about your body size?

113. How do you respond to comments about your body size from spouses or partners?

114. How did their attitudes about your body affect your relationship?

115. What are your thoughts and feelings about wearing a bathing suit?

116. Do you own a bathing suit? If not why?

117. Are the bathing suits you own the ones you actually want to wear?

118. How did you feel when you bought a bathing suit?

119. Describe a time when you didn't participate in activity because of your size.

120. Describe a time when you didn't wear something you wanted to because of your size.

121. Do you have any concerns/fears about losing weight?

122. What is your favorites piece of clothing? Why?

123. What type of clothing do you avoid the most? Why?

124. Do your weight issues influence the way you shop?

125. Do you plan to have plastic/cosmetic surgery once you've arrived at your goal weight?

126. What are some things you're waiting to do after you lose weight.

127. Why can't you do those things now?

128. What makes you feel good about yourself?

129. What makes you feel proud?

130. What kinds of situations make you feel comfortable?

131. Write a childhood memory about an incident related to your weight or body shape?

132. List some limiting beliefs you have that might be hindering your ability to lose weight.

133. Have you ever been discriminated against because of your weight?

134. What opportunities have you missed out on because of your size?

135. Where would you be right now if you were a healthy weight all your life?

136. Do you think your relationships would be the same if you were skinnier?

137. Do you think your life experiences would have changed if you were healthier?

138. Would your life have been completely different if you were thin for most of your life?

139. How will losing weight change your life situation?

140. Do you find yourself judging someone who is overweight?

141. Are your distracted by or condescending towards someone who is 100+ pounds overweight?

142. How do you feel when you see a morbidly obese person at a buffet or restaurant?

143. Is your weight keeping you from reaching your goals in life?

144. Do you think you're putting your life on hold because you want to lose weight first?

145. Who am I?

146. Who have I been?

147. Who do I want to be?

148. What do I want most in life? How can I get it?

149. What are my biggest barriers? Why do they block me?

150. How can I work on barriers?

151. What does an ideal body look like?

152. What does MY ideal body look like?

153. Describe a time when you were most satisfied with your body.

154. How did you look when you were most satisfied with your body?

155. How did you feel when you were most satisfied with your body?

156. How can you recreate these feelings?

157. If I could take a magic pill and have my dream body, what would it be?

158. Dear body, I love you because...

159. My body delightful because...

160. If it weren't for my body, I would...

161. What does body acceptance mean to me?

162. Today, I choose to love _____(insert body part), because _____.

163. I am more than my body because...

164. For me a beautiful person has...

165. If my body type were the current beauty ideal, I would ...So, what keeps me from doing this?

166. What's one small ritual/routine I can add to my life to change so I can be more self aware?

167. What is my life story through my body's eyes?

168. I am awesome because...

169. My best features are...

170. Here are all the things I've achieved in my life.

171. I am successful at...

172. I am really good at...

173. My cute quirks are...

174. My proudest moments are...

175. My most memorable experience was when...

176.	People say I am good at...

177.	What can I do better than most people?

178.	What parts of my body do I like and why?

179.	What parts of my body do I want to improve and why?

180.	In what ways am I aligned with my soul and my true self?

181.	What in my life feels off, heavy or draining?

182.	What areas of my life am I happiest with & why?

183.	When was a time that I listened to an intrusive pull from my soul— even if it didn't make practical sense — and it turned out amazing!

184.	Are my choices leading to my wholeheartedness, or do they leave me feeling empty and searching?

185.	What patterns or understandings can I see about myself?

LIFE CHANGING PROMPTS TO INSPIRE A HEALTHIER LIFESTYLE

"Just like your body and lifestyle can be healthy or unhealthy, the same is true with your beliefs. Your beliefs can be your medicine or your poison." —Steve Maraboli

186.   What does health mean to me?

187.   What prompted you to want to become healthier?

188.   What does a perfectly healthy day look like?

189.   What are you eating when you feel your best?

190.   What are you eating when you look your best?

191.   Make a list of short-term goals and long-term goals.

192.   Does planning a reward work for achieving your health goals?

193.   What rewards have you planned for achieving short term goals?

194.   What rewards have you planned for achieving your long term goals?

195.   Make a list of rewards you can give yourself that have nothing to do with food.

196.   What's the ultimate reward for achieving your goal weight?

197.   How will you maintain your goal weight?

198.   List the habits you're doing that are not helping your health.

199. Make a list of good habits you'd like to incorporate into your life.

200. What things are you doing to heal your body?

201. What am I doing to get at least 8 glasses of water a day?

202. What are my tips and tricks for incorporating more water into my diet?

203. What changes have I noticed that are attributed to drinking more water?

204. What unhealthy foods have I eliminated from my diet because I'm OK with never eating them again?

205. What foods do I not want to eliminate from my diet?

206. How can I achieve balance and harmony between what I want to eat and what I should eat?

207. Do you eat out often? Why?

208. Are you easily overwhelmed or intimidated by the food menu at restaurants?

209. What is your strategy for eating at restaurants?

210. What is your strategy for special occasions and holidays?

211. Are you logging your food into a diary?

212. Are you keeping track of what you're eating?

213. Do you enjoy logging your food or are you having trouble being consistent?

214. Do you think keeping a food diary is the key to successful weight loss?

215. How does being a parent affect your weight loss program?

216. List food items you usually eat for breakfast.

217. Is eating breakfast vital to your weight loss program? Why?

218. Do you think breakfast is the most important meal of the day?

219. What is the most important meal of the day and why?

220. What are 3 likes I have about losing weight?

221. What are 3 dislikes I have about losing weight?

222. What are all the methods of measuring health besides the number on the scale?

223. When was the last time you gave up your diet because your "weight loss" buddy gave up?

224. What do you need to do to overcome your dependence on another person for your health?

225. What is your ideal goal weight?

226. How many pounds do you need to lose in order to reach your goal weight?how will you do this?

227. Do you think your goal weight is complimentary to your body frame?

228. Describe your eating habits at mealtime.

229. Do you think you need to change your eating habits in order to lose weight and get healthy?

230. Where do you usually eat?

231. Do you think your current eating habits are helping you achieve your goals?

232. Do you think eating healthy is too expensive?

233. Do you think processed food is cheaper than whole-form foods?

234. Are you spending more money on food since starting your weight loss journey?

235. Do you think losing weight quickly is damaging to your health?

236. Is there a way to lose weight quickly and keep it off for good?

237. How do you feel about slow and steady weight loss?

238. What's best for you? Slow and steady weight loss as a lifestyle or quick weight loss for motivation and then maintain?

239. How do I measure success?

240. Has your idea of success changed since you made the decision to become healthier?

241. Do you have a "secret stash" of binge foods hidden somewhere?

242. What is the difference between a resolution and a goal?

243. What are some things you're doing differently in the present, now that you're more aware of your health?

244. What patterns can see that are hindering my healthy lifestyle?

245. What's one belief that is holding me back in life?

246. How can I replace limiting beliefs with abundant beliefs?

247. What can I do today to feel good in my body?

248. Despite everything, I know that my body needs...

249. Today I can treat my body better by...

250. If I were to experiment with feeling good in my body today, I would...

251. What does being "happy" mean to me?

252. How can I treat myself without using food?

253. What is the ultimate lifestyle I want to live?

254. What things am I taking for granted?

255. What is the beset advice I've ever received with regards to living a healthier lifestyle?

256. I wish I knew...because...

257. If I had to do it all over again, what would I change about my lifestyle?

258. What inspires me is...because...

259. Make a list of your favorite affirmations.

260. Make a list of your favorite quotes.

261. What do I think someone in good shape does in their free time?

262. What do I think someone in good shape eats all day?

263. What good lifestyle habit can I start today?

264. What do I want to do more of in life?

265. What do I want to do less of in life?

266. Am I giving my full attention and being present when I speak to the people around me?

267. Do I speak to myself the same way I speak to my friends?

268. How can I be kinder to myself?

269. If I had no obstacles for fear, what would I do with my life?

270. How can I be creative in solving the triggers that make me binge/overeat?

271. How can I be creative in solving the triggers that cause me to self sabotage?

272. What are 3 activities that make me happy and how often do I do these?

273. What is one thing I need more than anything?

274. When did I feel most alive? What was I doing? Who was I with?

275. This is a detailed description of my ideal life...

276. Am I simply reacting to life instead of taking my own initiative over life?

277. What is a habit I want to change?

278. What is a new habit I want to adopt into my life?

279. Am I making decisions out of fear of missing out or am I making decisions out of love & respect for my body?

280. What's one small ritual/routine I can add to my life to change the part of my life I'm least happy with?

281. What is 1 small action I can take today to live the life I want?

282. What is my definition of beauty?

283. What is beautiful about life?

284. Am I beautiful?

285. Am I waiting for something in life?

286. What is my ideal life like?

287. What are the traits of a person living a healthy lifestyle?

288. What is my top priority in life right now?

289. Do I care too much about what others think of me?

290. What do I need more of in my life?

291. What are my most favorite feelings? What things make these feelings arise?

292. Am I being my true self?

293. Are there ways in which I'm causing pain to myself?

294. How can I be more adventurous?

295. What do I believe about other people?

296. Is my perspective about others a healthy and loving perspective to have?

297. How am I the same as everyone else?

298. When is my most productive time of day? How can I utilize this time better?

299. What have I learned from my past mistakes?

300. What is something about myself that I keep in and never let others know about?

301. Are the thoughts I have throughout the day positive or negative?

302. What are 10 insecurities I have about myself?

303. Is there something I want to do that I think is impossible? How can I overcome my perception of impossibility?

304. Do I like change, do I adapt well to change?

305. What is my life purpose/goal?

306. What do I promise myself?

307. How can I create harmony in my life?

308. How has my lifestyle changed in the last 5 years?

309. What does family mean to me?

310. How can I help others?

311. What causes stress or anxiety in my life?

312. In what ways do I care for others?

313. What can I do to get enough sleep?

314. What is your perfect night time routine?

315. What is a night time routine that might help you sleep more soundly?

316. How can you promote better sleep in your life?

317. Do you feel that sleep is a waste of time? Why?

318. What are all the benefits of getting adequate sleep?

319. How can I be a more empathic person?

320. Do I focus on the present enough?

321. What kind of person do I want to be in the future?

322. Make a bucket list.

323. Make a "places to travel to" list.

324. Do I compare myself to others? How can I stop doing this?

325. What are some things I want to have/buy? Why?

326. Do I eat healthy and exercise enough? How can adopt a more healthy lifestyle?

327. Do I feel uncomfortable in my own skin? Why?

328. How can I become more comfortable with the uncomfortable?

329. What is the best piece of lifestyle advice I've ever been given?

330. What patterns do I see that are helping my healthy lifestyle?

INSIGHTFUL PROMPTS TO LEVEL UP YOUR NUTRITION KNOWLEDGE

"Today more than 95% of all chronic disease is caused by food choice, toxic food ingredients, nutritional deficiencies, and lack of physical exercise." — Mike Adams

331. What do I know about nutrition?

332. What consists of a balanced and healthy meal?

333. Am I eating well?

334. How much am I eating everyday?

335. Are there voids in my nutrition that might be causing weight gain?

336. What am I doing correctly, in providing my body with nutrition?

337. A list of books I've read on nutrition.

338. A list of resources I go to for nutrition information.

339. Do a book review on a nutrition book you've read.

340. What is my favorite book on nutrition and why?

341. Are weight loss and nutrition the same thing?

342. Name all the books you've read on weight loss.

343. Do a book review on a weight loss book you've read.

344. What is your favorite weight loss theory and why?

345. List all the fresh vegetables and fruits that are on your food plan.

346. How many servings of vegetables and fruit do you consume every day

347. Why should we eat balanced meals?

348. What are whole foods?

349. How can I eat more whole foods?

350. How will I prepare my food so that it's consumed as close to its original form as possible?

351. Are condiments necessary?

352. What are healthy condiment choices?

353. What condiments can I throw out?

354. How can I keep my food preparation simple?

355. How will eating healthily now affect your body in the future?

356. What do you think of when you think about healthy foods?

357. Is there anything about nutrition that you would like to learn more about?

358. How could you eat more healthily?

359. Why do our bodies need nutrition?

360. How can people with little access to food be properly nourished?

361. Do you ever cook with your family?

362. Describe a day of your normal meals.

363. How do you feel after eating a healthy meal?

364. If you could make your own balanced diet, what would it include?

365. What is your favorite healthy food?

366. How much water do you drink each day?

367. How do you feel when you think of animals as food?

368. Do you prefer fruit or vegetables? Why?

369. Could you ever be a vegetarian?

370. How does a person's diet affect his or her overall health?

371. What is your favorite food group?

372. Are diet and exercise both important? Is one more important than the other?

373. Does you have any special dietary rules?

374. What are some of your favorite healthy snacks?

375. Do you mostly eat a balanced diet?

376. What are the food groups?

377. What tips for healthy eating would you give to someone interested in changing his or her diet?

378. When is it okay to have treats?

379. How often do you eat during the day?

380. Record everything you eat for a week. What do you notice about your eating habits?

381. Are there any foods you eat just because they are healthy?

382. How does nutrition influence wellness?

383. Do you eat until you're full or until your plate is clear?

384. Should anything in your normal diet change?

385. What do you do when you encounter foods you don't like?

386. Do you get to choose what you eat?

387. If you had to eat fruit or vegetables every day for the rest of your life, which would you choose?

388. How can you inject more color into your diet?

389. Write a poem about the importance of eating healthily.

390. Why doesn't junk food grow on trees?

391. Would you rather be a vegetarian or a vegan?

392. What is your favorite meal?

393. How often do you eat meat?

394. How do you feel when you eat too many sweets?

395. How do Americans eat differently than people in other countries?

396. Why is hydration important?

397. Does your family eat meals together?

398. Why are processed foods unhealthy?

399. Do you know of any alternate ways to get nutrients?

400. Why do you want to eat healthily?

401. What are five ways you could improve your overall diet?

402. Do you think you're eating enough fruits and vegetable?

403. How do you think you can incorporate more fruits and vegetables into your daily consumption?

404. What kinds of foods did you mainly eat as a child?

405. What kinds of foods do you mainly eat now?

406. List some personal tips and tricks for getting in all your fruits and vegetables.

407. Do you serve yourself different food than you serve your family? Why?

408. Do you often go to the store with the best intention not to buy junk food, but when you get to the car, your bags are full of them?

409. Do you stick to a shopping list of nutritious foods?

410. Are you often "hangry" when trying to lose weight?

411. Do you avoid impulse aisles when grocery shopping?

412. List your secrets for staying on course with your food shopping trips.

413. How does eating healthy make you feel?

414. What are your thoughts and feelings about eating more nutritious meals?

415. Do you think nutritious meals are satisfying?

416. List the foods you like to eat that are also nutritious and good for you.

417. What was the best thing about your weight loss program in the past?

418. What was the worst thing about your weight loss program in the past?

419. What's worked before as far as healthy goes?

420. What's not worked before as far as eating healthy goes?

421. Do you think low carb is healthy?

422. Think of any popular diet. What are the pros and cons of using that technique?

423. Do diets have to be strict?

424. Will having everything in moderation keep you from losing weight?

425. What is the healthiest diet?

426. What is your ideal diet?

427. What are some tools I use in the kitchen that help me live a healthier lifestyle?

428. What kitchen tools can I not live without that make cooking healthy easier?

429. What do I most want for my body?

430. How will I achieve the things I want the most for my body?

431. How do I connect food and body?

432. What are my biggest daily challenges with food?

433. Today, I can feed my body better by.

434. 10 reasons why I should eat healthier.

435. Is fat loss and weight loss the same thing?

436. What are some ways I can lose fat?

437. How can I eat to lose fat?

438. What are the essential nutrients my body needs to function optimally?

439. What do I need to eat to give my body the essential nutrients it needs?

440. Would I rather eat 6 small meals a day or 3 regular meals a day?

441. How do I feel about cheat days?

442. How do I feel about fasting?

443. Are carbohydrates bad for you?

444. What types of fat are good for me? How I can incorporate more of these into my meals?

445. What types of fat are bad for me? How can I stop eating these?

446. Are potatoes bad for me?

447. Do I *need* to eat meat?

448. Does my body need carbs?

449. How much protein do I *really* need?

450. What are plant based sources of protein I should eat?

451. What are plant based carbohydrates I should eat?

452. What are the ideal portion sizes I should be eating.

453. What are foods I can eat in unlimited amounts and still be healthy?

454. What are foods that make me feel really good and well?

455. What are foods that I regularly eat that make be feel really bad and unhealthy? Why do I still eat them?

456. What is something that's really worked for my health and nutrition in the past?

457. What type of dieter am I?

458. Are diet and nutrition the same thing?

459. What are calories?

460.   Is counting calories effective for losing fat?

461.   What are my favorite foods to eat?

462.   Can I lose weight while eating my favorite foods? How?

463.   Do I *need* to give up all my favorite foods in order to lose weight?

464.   Do I *want* to give up my favorite foods in the name of weight loss?

465.   What are some foods I know are bad for me, that I can give up and never miss?

466.   What are some super nutritious foods I don't really like but I'll eat them because I know they give my body the nutrients it needs.

467.   What are some super nutritious foods I like to eat?

468.   How can I creatively eat incorporate my favorite foods into my diet plan?

469.   What are my favorite drinks to drink?

470.   Is eating the fruit healthier or drinking the fruit juice healthier?

471.   Do I believe that my body will go into starvation mode if I fast for 12 hours?

472.   Is there such a thing as starvation mode?

473.   What is a ritual/routine I can add to my life so I can be more nutritious?

474.   What expectations have I put on my nutrition? Are they realistic?

475. These are the excuses I've made for not eating healthy...

476. Here's a fruit or vegetable that I've never had before. I will buy it, cook it and eat it. I will write about it here.

477. Write about a food fad I tried and why it didn't work.

478. What are some ridiculous ways I've tried to lose weight?

479. What are some things I've eaten to lose weight that I hated?

480. What do I think a healthy person eats all day?

481. What good nutrition habit can I start now?

482. Are my choices aligned with how I want my body to look and feel?

483. Do I feel good about what I choose to put in my body?

484. Do I have full control over what I eat?

485. What is an eating habit I want to change?

486. What is a new eating habit I want to adopt?

487. What is the best piece of nutrition advice I've ever been given? Do I follow that advice?

488. Who is a healthy person I admire? What about them is so admirable?

489. How can I be creative in solving the problems that compel me to eat unhealthy food?

490. In 3 words, how would I describe the type of person I want to be?

491. Describe in one paragraph how healthy you are.

492. What is 1 small action I can take today to eat healthier?

493. To what extent (if any) is being overweight influenced by our genes?

494. What patterns or understandings can I see about my nutrition?

MOVING PROMPTS THAT ACTIVATE ENERGY AND ACTIVITY

"Movement is medicine for creating change in a person's physical, emotional and mental states." —Carol Welch

495.   What is fitness?

496.   How can I become for fit?

497.   What counts as exercise?

498.   How can I start small and build my strength and stamina?

499.   How do I feel about exercise? Why?

500.   How have I incorporated exercise as a regular part of my life?

501.   List at least 10 physical activities that I *could* do.

502.   List all the physical activities that I really *like* to do.

503.   Where are the places I like to exercise? Gym? Outdoors? Home?

504.   What kind of exercise did I do when I was younger? Do I still do those things now? Why or why not?

505.   Do I love or hate exercise? Why?

506.   Do I like my current exercise program?

507.   Things I can do to make exercise more exciting?

508.   How do I feel before a workout?

509. How do I feel after I've had a really good workout?

510. How do I feel knowing that I should exercise for the rest of my life?

511. What are my thoughts when I see really fit people?

512. What do I think really fit people are doing to get fit?

513. Do I have dedicate my life to working out to get fit? Why?

514. Is it impossible for me to get fit?

515. What is holding me back from my fitness?

516. Here's why it's absolutely possible for my body to get fit.

517. What is my body capable of now?

518. What *could* my body be capable of?

519. Did you have PE in school? Did you like or hate it?

520. Are you athletically inclined?

521. Have you ever participated in a team sport? Did you like it and why?

522. Do you like individual sports more than team sports why?

523. What sports have you tried?

524. What sports would you like to try/learn?

525. What is physical strength to me?

526. What am I doing when I am strongest?

527. Do you enjoy/are you easily inspired from watching sports?

528. What were my hobbies as a child?

529. What are my hobbies now?

530. Are the things you generally like to do activity based or passive based?

531. What are new hobbies I can start that are activity based?

532. Who is your favorite fitness influencer and why?

533. How often do you weight yourself?

534. Does the number on the scale matter?

535. Are weight loss and fat loss the same?

536. What are some other methods of measuring fat loss?

537. When was the last time you gave up exercise because your "diet buddy" gave up?

538. What do you need to do to overcome dependence on another person for being active?

539. What do you think about when you exercise?

540. How can you make exercise more pleasant?

541. Does exercise only mean rigorous activity?

542. Does yoga constitute as exercise? Why or why not?

543. What is your favorite exercise playlist? How does it make you feel?

544. Think about your favorite exercise attire. Why do you like it so much?

545. List all the tools you need to have an ideal exercise experience.

546. How can I invest time for exercise this year?

547. List all the ways exercise can be beneficial to you.

548. What is a habit I want to change when it comes to exercise?

549. What is an exercise habit I want to adopt into my life?

550. What can exercise do for you mentally?

551. What can exercise do you physically?

552. How can exercise enhance your life?

553. If my body were magic, it would...

554. When do I feel best in my body?

555. What exercises do I want to try?

556. What activities make me lose track of time?

557. What exercises always improve my mood?

558. What is standing between me and my ideal fitness?

559. What does happiness feel like in my body?

560.   What does strength feel like in my body?

561.   What do I want to change about my exercise habits? How do I achieve that?

562.   What do I want to change about my physicality? How will I do that?

563.   What expectations have I put on my fitness regimen? Are they realistic?

564.   Is my fitness regimen something I can enjoy and look forward to?

565.   Is my fitness regimen something I can see myself doing for a long time?

566.   Who is my fitness role model and why?

567.   Is the fitness regimen that I've planned for myself what I really want?

568.   What fitness activities activities do I see myself doing for years to come?

569.   These are the excuses I've made for not exercising.

570.   What is my greatest physical achievement?

571.   When do I feel most alive?

572.   What's one small ritual/routine I can add to my life so that I can get more exercise?

573.   What is something I can do now that I couldn't do before?

574.   How can you encourage others to exercise?

575. What benefits do you share when you exercise with others?

576. Why is exercise so important?

577. Do you like exercising indoors or outdoors better?

578. What is your favorite part of exercise?

579. After I exercise, I feel...

580. Would you rather take a long walk or a short run? What are the benefits of each?

581. How often do you exercise?

582. Come up with three ways you can make exercise more fun.

583. How does good nutrition relate to exercise?

584. Make a list of five small ways you can be more active and write about their importance.

585. What is your favorite sport that gets you moving?

586. What do you know about the benefits of exercise?

587. What is your favorite way to exercise?

588. How does living an active lifestyle help you to appreciate your mobility?

589. What are some ways to make exercise even more fun?

590. What is your exercise commitment? How will you keep it?

591. Describe your ideal workout routine.

592. How many days each week are you active?

593. What does it mean to have an active lifestyle?

594. How can you make time for exercise each day?

595. How can you involve your family in exercise?

596. What do you think of when you think of exercise?

597. Do you like listening to music while you exercise? What kind? How does it make you feel?

598. How does your body feel after you exercise?

599. What emotions do you feel when you exercise?

600. Do you think people exercise enough?Is it more important to exercise or eat right – or both?

601. Do you exercise with your family or by yourself?

602. How do you feel when you go a long time without exercising?

603. How does your pet help you to exercise?

604. What are some surprising ways to get exercise?

605. Write about the best workout you ever had.

606. What are some good exercises to do inside when it gets cold or rainy?

607. What are your favorite active things to do outside when it's warm?

608. The best part of exercising is...

609. Make a week-long exercise schedule to follow.

610. What are some of the largest benefits of exercise?

611. What is your favorite kind of exercise machine?

612. Do you prefer getting active by playing team sports or individual ones?

613. How can exercise be a good time to connect with your family?

614. What is the most important thing you've learned about exercise?

615. What time of day do you like to exercise?

616. Is exercise important to your family?

617. Think of ten active things you can do with your family.

618. Do you believe exercise is important? How can you implement this belief into your life?

619. What exercise do I wish I would've spent more time learning 5 years ago?

620. What fitness fad did I try that I absolutely hated?

621. Who is a fit person I admire? What about them is so admirable?

622. What good exercise habits can I start right now?

623. What is 1 small action I can take today, to get more exercise?

624. What is the best piece of exercise advice I've ever been given? Am I following that advice?

625. Am I being adventurous enough?

626. Am I stretching before I exercise?

627. Do I regularly do stretching exercises?

628. How much exercise does my body need?

629. What does it mean when someone says, "you cannot out exercise a bad diet"? What point are they trying to prove?

630. What workout can I do in only 15 minutes?

631. What workout can I do in in 30 minutes?

632. Where in my current schedule can I fit in 15 minutes of activity?

633. Where in my current schedule can I fit in 30 minutes of activity?

634. Am I taking the time to recover after a workout?

635. How do I recover after a workout?

636. What should I eat or drink after I workout?

637. What cardio should I do?

638. What does it mean when the scale says I'm heavier, yet my body fat is less?

639. What types of cardio do I find fun and enjoyable?

640. What is the most convenient way for me to get more exercise?

641. How can I be creative in solving the problems that keep me from exercising?

642. List all the reasons you should exercise besides to weight.

POWERFUL PROMPTS THAT SPARK SELF CARE

"Nourishing yourself in a way that helps you blossom in the direction you want to go is attainable, and you are worth the effort" —Deborah Day

643. What makes me improve my mood?

644. What are everyday things that make me happy?

645. What does happiness mean?

646. Make a list of 100 things that makes you happy. Include the smallest things.

647. When was the last time I was feeling ecstatic and why?

648. What is standing between me and my happiness?

649. What are indulgent things I can do that have nothing to do with food?

650. How can I treat myself without spending any money?

651. How can I treat myself without eating?

652. How can I express love to myself

653. How do I express love to someone else?

654. What is going well in my life right now?

655. What does imperfection mean to me?

656. How do I accept imperfections in others?

657. How can I become more selfish?

658. What can I say no to more often?

659. I love me because...

660. How can I do more of what makes me happy?

661. How can cut out things that make me unhappy?

662. What is a good self care habit I can commit to starting now?

663. How can I accept imperfections in myself?

664. I am awesome because ...

665. What is your biggest struggle with loving yourself?

666. Am I taking enough care of myself?

667. Get rid of a limiting belief that you have about yourself or your abilities.

668. What good habit do you want to begin this month?

669. What's one compliment you struggle to accept about yourself?

670. What do you need to start saying "yes" to?

671. What do i need to start saying "no" to?

672. What do you need to forgive yourself for?

673. Write a letter to older you.

674. Write a letter to younger you.

675. How can I be a calmer person?

676.   What do I love to do for fun?

677.   Why is beautiful about life?

678.   Name a thing that you love about your body and then a thing you love about your personality.

679.   Where in your life do you need to slow down and take your time?

680.   What's something that you need to get rid of?

681.   How can you set better boundaries in your life?

682.   How would you describe yourself, in a loving way, to a stranger?

683.   What things make you feel happy to be alive? And how can you add MORE of that into your life?

684.   Take a selfie just as you are. Write a description of your face using loving words.

685.   What would your younger self be proud of you for today?

686.   What are you afraid to ask for? What do you need to speak up about?

687.   What is the most loving thing you've ever done for yourself?

688.   When was the last time you indulged yourself and how?

689.   What's one change in your life that you can make for more happiness?

690.   How am I making the world a better place?

691. Is there something or someone I need to forgive in life?

692. Am I forgiving myself enough?

693. How can you give yourself a break today? [Mentally, physically, or emotionally]

694. What's something that you're working on believing that you deserve?

695. What things make you feel bad, but you find yourself doing them anyway?

696. What does your support system look like? How can you make it stronger?

697. What's something you wish someone would say to you?

698. What things are you really really good at?

699. What's one choice you can make right now that your future self will thank you for?

700. Who are your role models and what qualities do you (already) share with them?

701. What words or beliefs do you (want to) live your life by?

702. What labels, negative and positive, do you assign yourself?

703. Going forward, how can you commit to loving yourself every day?

704. Two words phrases that make me laugh

705. How can I make time for things that bring me the most joy?

706. What do I need to get off my chest today?

707. How can I simplify my life in little ways?

708. What advice should I give to myself right now?

709. How do I relax?

710. What do I feel strongly about?

711. What are my priorities in life?

712. Five things I need to do less often.

713. How can I be more content?

714. One way I would like to grow next year.

715. What is something new I want to learn?

716. Write a poem you love.

717. What makes me unique?

718. How can I be kinder to myself?

719. Do I treat myself the same way I treat my loved ones?

720. What would I be doing if money wasn't an object?

721. What's one thing I can do daily, to stop and give myself a 5 minute break?

722. How can I be creative in solving the problems that compel me to not take good care of myself?

723.   What's on my mind right now?

724.   What is 1 small action I can take today for self care?

725.   What is something I've always wanted to do?

726.   What are my most favorite things to do?

727.   What are 10 things in my life right now that make me happy?

728.   List all the things that I can do do make myself happy.

729.   What is the meaning of love?

730.   How can I be a more loving person to others and to myself?

731.   Do I apologize enough?

732.   Do I apologize too often?

733.   What can I do for me, to make my life more meaningful?

734.   Am I taking care of myself enough?

735.   What can I be doing more for self care?

736.   What makes me sad?

737.   What is a secret I should confess?

738.   What is something I want to do tomorrow?

739.   What is the best piece of self care advice I've ever been given? Do I follow that advice?

740.   What is a ritual/routine I can add to my life for self care?

EFFECTIVE PROMPTS FOR CLARITY IN OVERCOMING SETBACKS

"Give yourself a break. Stop beating yourself up! Everyone makes mistakes, has setbacks and failures. You don't come with a book on how to get it right all the time. You will fail sometimes, not because you planned to, but simply because you're human. Failure is part of creating a great life. Stand up to it and handle it with grace. Because you can." — Les Brown

741.   Do holidays set back your weight loss program? What can you do about it?

742.   Do weekends set back your weight loss program? What can you do about it?

743.   List ways you can "bounce back" after the holidays.

744.   What are your strategies for getting back on track?

745.   What are your strategies to prevent giving up?

746.   What happened the last time you gave up?

747.   How can you tailor your diet to work for you now?

748.   Make a list of people who can support you in your weight loss program

749.   Make a list of people you can become healthier with.

750.   Do you find that weight loss is easier with people or do you like to keep your efforts private? Why?

751.   List the things you didn't like about weight loss programs you tried in the past.

752. List the things you liked about weight loss programs you tried in the past.

753. Do you think there is a perfect diet?

754. Do you think you can map out your own "perfect" diet?

755. What will the perfect diet consist of?

756. What are your goals and plans?

757. Health wise, what were your accomplishments in the past?

758. Health wise what were your disappointments in the past?

759. What are all the excuses you've made in the past for giving up on your diet?

760. What's the craziest excuse you've made for getting "off the wagon"?

761. Whats the most outrageous comment you've received about your weight loss?

762. What's the goofiest diet tip you've ever received?

763. What's the weirdest weigh-in ritual you've ever heard of or done?

764. What keeps you going, even after falling off the wagon?

765. When happened the last time you felt you hit a wall.

766. Why do you think there are weight loss plateaus?

767. Why do people give up losing weight?

768. What do you do after you've fallen off the wagon?

769. What motivates you to get back on your diet and exercise regimen?

770. What's the best kick in the butt for getting back on track?

771. How can you overcome a plateau?

772. Where do I practice forgiveness in my life?

773. What are some things that I can give more to and still be happy?

774. What gives me pleasure and joy?

775. What in my life makes me feel alive and energized?

776. I feel most at peace and connected when I... because...

777. Write a letter of advice to younger me about setbacks.

778. What advice would older me tell the "now" me?

779. What am I most looking forward to?

780. How can I be different 1 year from now?

781. What do I wish I'd done differently?

782. What would be different now if I never gave up?

783. What went super well in the past? How do I replicate it?

784. What is different now because of my successes?

785. What words do I wish someone would say to me right now?

786. What do I know now that I didn't know before about setbacks?

787. How do I overcome setbacks?

788. How can I give the things I want to myself?

789. 10 favorites quotes I have about setbacks.

790. Who is somebody I admire and what was their biggest failure? How did they bounce back?

791. Do you have hero? Why are they your hero?

792. What are some pep talks I like to give myself?

793. What does having momentum mean to me?

794. When did I take my biggest leap of faith?

795. How can I be creative in solving the problems that compel me to give up?

796. Let's take a look back at how far I've come.

797. What is a ritual/routine I can add to my life to keep me from giving up?

798. What is 1 small action I can make to keep me from giving up?

799. What is the best piece of advice I've been given for not giving up? Do I follow that advice?

800.   What patterns can I see about myself and giving up?

UPLIFTING PROMPTS THAT INCREASE
HAPPINESS THROUGH GRATITUDE

"Gratitude unlocks the fullness of life. It turns what we have into enough, and more. It turns denial into acceptance, chaos to order, confusion to clarity. It can turn a meal into a feast, a house into a home, a stranger into a friend." —Melody Beattie

801. I am grateful for...

802. Today, I am grateful for...

803. I am grate for my body because...

804. Parts of my body I am grateful for...

805. I am grateful that my body can...

806. What are 3 things I love about myself?

807. What are some things that make me smile?

808. Here is a list of my favorite foods.

809. What is my favorite photo? Why?

810. What do I love most about nature?

811. Make a list of all the things your body as achieved.

812. I am grateful for my healthy heart because...

813. What was the best part of my day today?

814. What am I most looking forward to right now

815. What was the last act of kindness that was done for me?

816. Who is the most important person in my life?

817. I am really great at...

818. The last time I laughed really hard was when...

819. An accomplishment I am most proud of is...

820. What if my favorite scent? What memories does it invoke?

821. What is my favorite tradition?

822. My favorite teacher was...

823. The most thoughtful gift I've ever been given is...

824. The part of my weekly routine I look forward to the most is...

825. A place that always brings me happy memories is...

826. A simple pleasure I'm grateful for is...

827. What's something I'm grateful to have today that I didn't have a year ago?

828. Write about a happy memory.

829. What is a possession that makes your life easier?

830. What's something or someone that makes you feel safe?

831. How are you able to help other?

832. What about a friend am I grateful for?

833. What did I accomplish today?

834. What mistakes or failures am I grateful for?

835. What's something I was able to buy that I'm grateful for?

836. Who would I be unable to live without?

837. What are the sounds I can hear right now?

838. What do I feel when hear the word "freedom"?

839. What smell do you love smelling the most?

840. Which emotion is your favorite to experience?

841. How does the holiday season make you feel?

842. Did a teacher influence your life in a positive way?

843. What have you learned from unpleasant emotions?

844. Who is the most positive, inspiring person you know?

845. What quote made you think about life differently?

846. Which animals have positively impacted your life?

847. How do you feel about your closest friends?

848. What is your favorite physical trait?

849. Who was the last person you hugged?

850. What traditions did you enjoy as a child?

851. Did you learn any lessons from a childhood friend?

852. Where did you rest your head last night?

853. What opportunities have changed your life?

854. How do you like to spend your spare time?

855. What three things do you see in front of you?

856. What do you enjoy about your career?

857. How does it feel to wake up every single day?

858. When was the last vacation you went on?

859. What is the best thing you've ever read?

860. How has technology impacted your life?

861. What character traits are you happy to have?

862. When did you last feel pure excitement?

863. How do you feel in your favorite outfit?

864. When was the last time you laughed really hard?

865. What TV show do you enjoy watching?

866. How did it feel the first time you fell in love?

867. What is your favorite or best talent?

868. Do you have a simple pleasure you really enjoy?

869. What luxury are you lucky to have access to?

870. How did it feel to leave a bad situation?

871. Who did you last say "I love you" to?

872. What inspires you to keep going when it's hard?

873. Who provides you with a valuable service?

874. What is the best gift you have ever received?

875. Do you have a favorite memory?

876. How does it feel to get paid for your work?

877. What color makes you feel happiest?

878. Do you feel excited about your future?

879. What is one thing you're really proud of?

880. How do you express your love to others?

881. When was the last walk you went on?

882. What is your all-time favorite song?

883. How does it feel to eat a really great meal?

884. Do you have running water at home?

885. When did you last feel really cozy?

886. What kind of artwork makes you happy?

887. When did you last look up at the stars?

888. How does the sky above you look today?

889. What website do you enjoy visiting?

890. Do you enjoy traveling to new places?

891. When did you last lie in the sunshine?

892. How does it feel to give a gift?

893. When were you last encouraged/praised?

894. What's the most fun day you've had?

895. How do you enjoy your favorite month?

896. When were you last really surprised?

897. What's the best compliment you've received?

898. What are you really passionate about?

899. Do you enjoy a good dance party?

900. What have you learned recently?

901. How do you feel in moments spent alone?

902. What kindnesses have I experienced?

903. How does a good night's sleep feel?

904. What dessert do you most enjoy eating?

905. When did you last feel really at peace?

906. How do I recover from an illness?

907. When was the last time I forgave someone else?

908. When did someone else forgive me?

909. Where is my favorite place to be?

910. What do I love most about life?

911. What are different ways of showing gratitude?

912. What's one thing I can do for someone else today to show my appreciation for them?

913. What is 1 small action I can take today to express my gratitude for everything that I am blessed with.

914. What is a ritual/routine I can add to my life for showing or feeling gratitude?

THOUGHTFUL PROMPTS FOR CULTURE AND WEIGHT BIAS

"Health is a large word. It embraces not the body only, but the mind and spirit as well;...and not today's pain or pleasure alone, but the whole being and outlook of a man" —James H. West

915.   Why is childhood obesity on the rise?

916.   What are the main contributing factors to the increased rate of childhood obesity in your country?

917.   What are the main health effects of childhood obesity in later life?

918.   What can be done to a child's youth to help them stay fit into adulthood?

919.   How can we prevent weight problems in children?

920.   Are there more or fewer healthier eating options available now?

921.   How can we encourage everyone to go out and enjoy nature more?

922.   What should we as a society work on first? Fast food or lack of activity?

923.   Are obese parents more likely to have obese children?

924.   What is the social stigma attached to youth with weight issues?

925.   Does breastfeeding have any relation to weight issues in children?

926. What is the best way to prevent obesity in youth?

927. Why is the population getting fatter?

928. Why is type 2 diabetes more prevalent now compared to 40 years ago?

929. How has our diet changed over time?

930. What did our ancestors eat?

931. What did people eat 100 years ago?

932. What did people eat 50 years ago?

933. How do food companies increase their profits?

934. What are all the different names for sugar that food companies use?

935. Is milk really that good for you?

936. Have you ever been on farm? How do you feel about eating those animals?

937. Why do you think food processing plants are always in the middle of nowhere?

938. Do you know where the food you buy really comes from?

939. Find the source of exactly where the food you're eating comes from.

940. Are Europeans healthier and better looking? Why?

941. Why are the size of airplane seats so small?

942. Write about your most recent airplane ride.

943. How does traveling by plane make you feel about your body?

944. What are your thoughts and feelings about Hollywood's standards on what an actress should look like?

945. What are thoughts and feelings on what the media has portrayed as attractive and desired?

946. What is the most desired body type right now?

947. How has the image of an ideal body type changed in the past century?

948. The issue of obesity is back in the headlines from time to time...what are your thoughts on a fat tax?

949. Do you think that food companies announcing they will make their food products healthier by modifying certain ingredients will help make a difference in our battle against obesity?

950. Why are there such a proliferation of diet blogs on the internet?

951. Why do a large percentage of diet blogs disappear into cyberspace and never return ever again?

952. Why do we rarely see one achieve his or her goal weight while in "active blogging status?"

953. What are healthier societies doing differently?

954. Why are Americans so unhealthy?

955. Why are some societies who used to be healthier now experiencing heart disease, obesity and diabetes more than before?

956. What causes obesity?

957. Do you believe obesity is an epidemic in our country?

958. Does the fast food industry play a role in obesity?

959. Should fast food companies be held responsible for people being overweight?

960. Is there such a thing as food addiction?

961. How do you cure food addiction?

962. Does our society place too much stress on looking perfect?

963. Does our society place too much stress on being the right size?

964. Do you think more stores should offer plus sized clothing?

965. Is it unhealthy to be overweight?

966. Is it better to be overweight vs. being obese?

967. Does our society favor those who are thin?

968. Does our society dehumanize those who are fat?

969. Do you think weight stigma exists?

970. What is fatphobia?

971. How much is spent on stomach alteration surgery every year?

972. Why do people do stomach alteration surgery?

973. What comes to mind when you think of fat people?

974. What comes to mind when you think of thin people?

975. Are overweight people treated differently than their thinner counterparts?

976. How are overweight people treated differently?

977. How can we as a society encourage people to be comfortable in their own skin?

978. When was the first time you noticed there was a difference in the way fat and thin people are treated?

979. Do the people around you make comments about other people's sizes?

980. Do the people around you make comments about other people's weight fluctuations?

981. Why do people say, "oh you look great! Have you lost weight?"

982. Why do people never say, "oh you look great! Have. You gained weight?"

983. Does losing weight have a lot to do with looking great?

984. Do you associate thin people with anything in particular when it comes to ability?

985. Are thin people able to do certain things better than people who are not thin?

986. Are thin people more active?

987. What is skinny fat?

988. Can you be skinny and unhealthy?

989. Can you be fat and healthy?

990. What are the eating habits of thin people?

991. Do thin people have health problems?

992. If you are a thin person, are you afraid of gaining weight?

993. If you are overweight, are you afraid of getting fatter?

994. What can fat people not do? Why can't they?

995. What is body positivity?

996. Why are there 60 different names for sugar?

997. What does "natural flavoring" mean?

998. What are the biggest secrets food companies are hiding from us?

999. Do you think fat women who are body positive truly love their body?

1000. Does wanting to lose weight mean you hate your body?

CONCLUSION

I hope this list of 1000 journal prompts, has helped you on your weight loss or health betterment journey.

If this compilation of prompts has helped you write insightful entries in your own health journal and assisted you on your way to living a life filled with health and self exploration, **please take 2 minutes to write an honest review on the Amazon page**.

Reviews will help others embarking on a similar journey to yours, find this book so it can help them too. So pay it forward and let others know about this amazing resource.

Thank you and take care...*Always*.

"YOU CAN'T GO BACK AND CHANGE THE BEGINNING, BUT YOU CAN START WHERE YOU ARE AND CHANGE THE ENDING." —C.S. LEWIS

www.elevateyourdiet.com

Made in the USA
Monee, IL
23 December 2024

75274053R00052